D1681534

Published by Creative Paperbacks
P.O. Box 227, Mankato, Minnesota 56002
Creative Paperbacks is an imprint of
The Creative Company
www.thecreativecompany.us

Design and production by The Design Lab
Art direction by Rita Marshall
Printed by Corporate Graphics
in the United States of America

Photographs by 123RF (cbpix, Kristian Sekulic),
Alamy (Mark Conlin, Stephen Frink Collection),
Corbis (Ralph A. Clevenger), Dreamstime
(Afarusi119, Melvinlee), Getty Images (Brandon
Cole, Stephen Marks, Brian J. Skerry), iStockphoto
(Don Bayley, Dave Raboin), Minden Pictures
(Fred Bavendam)

Copyright © 2010 Creative Paperbacks
International copyright reserved in all countries.
No part of this book may be reproduced in any
form without written permission from the publisher.

The Library of Congress has cataloged the hardcover
edition as follows:
Bodden, Valerie.
Sharks / by Valerie Bodden.
p. cm. — (Amazing animals)
Includes bibliographical references and index.
Summary: A basic exploration of the appearance,
behavior, and habitat of sharks, the feared fishes
of the sea. Also included is a story from folklore
explaining why sharks have a bump on their heads.
ISBN 978-1-58341-812-3 (hardcover)
ISBN 978-0-89812-744-7 (pbk)
1. Sharks—Juvenile literature. I. Title. II. Series.
QL638.9.B625 2010
597.3—dc22   2009002715

CPSIA: 042412 PO1568

9 8 7 6 5 4

AMAZING ANIMALS
SHARKS
BY VALERIE BODDEN

CREATIVE PAPERBACKS

Sharks swim in oceans all around the world

Sharks are a kind of fish. There are about 375 different kinds of sharks in the world. People are still **discovering** new kinds of sharks.

discovering finding for the first time

5

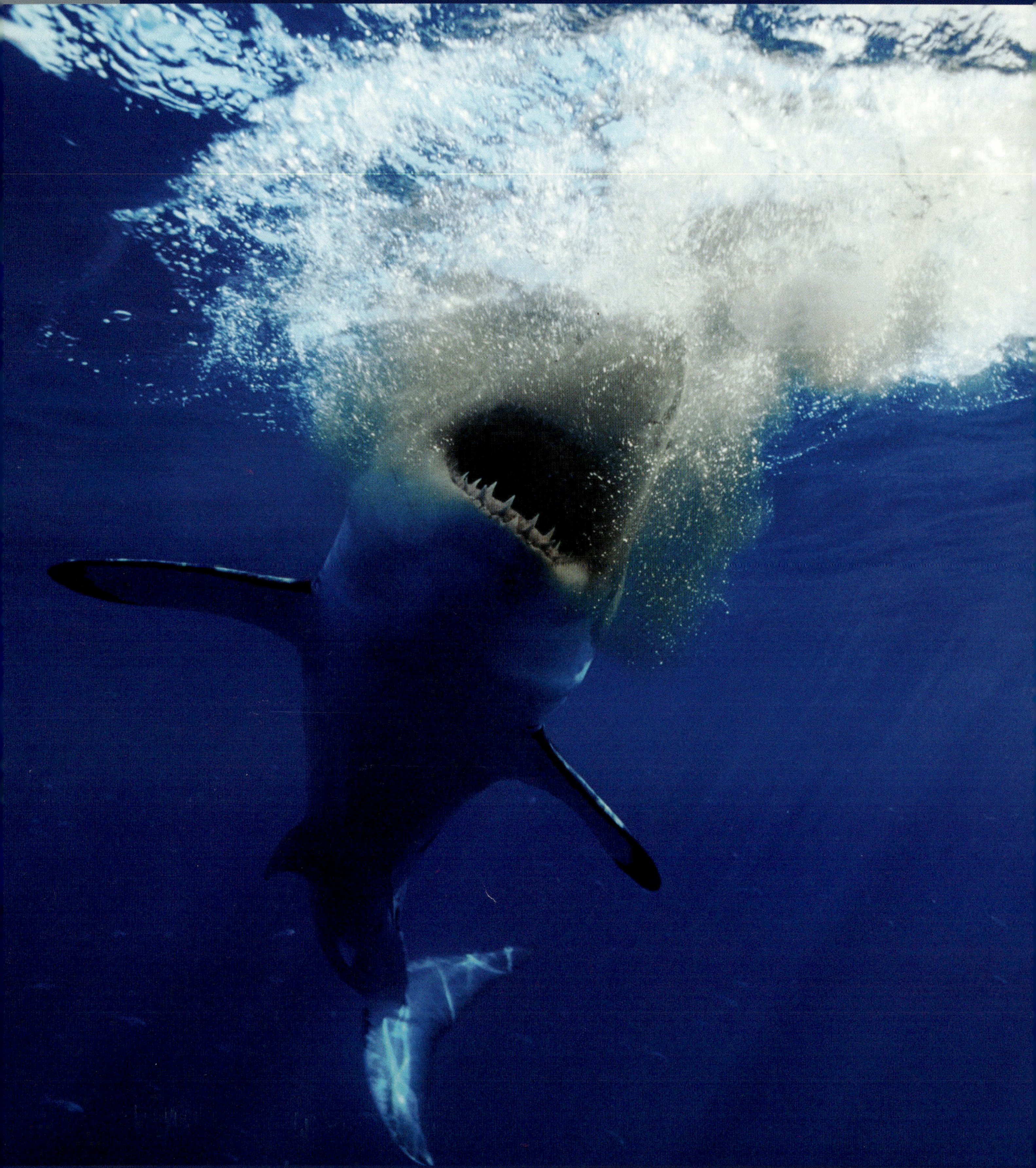

Sharks have rows of sharp teeth and gills

Sharks can be many colors. Some sharks are dark or spotted. Others are blue, gray, or white. Sharks' bodies are made of **cartilage** (CAR-*til-ij*) instead of bones. Sharks have lots of teeth. They breathe through slits in their sides called gills.

cartilage a tough, stretchy material in the body; people have cartilage in their nose and ears

Sharks come in different sizes.

The smallest sharks are the size of a kid's hand. The biggest shark is the whale shark. It is longer than a bus! Whale sharks can weigh 20 tons (18 t). That is more than two elephants put together!

The big whale shark eats only tiny fish and animals

9

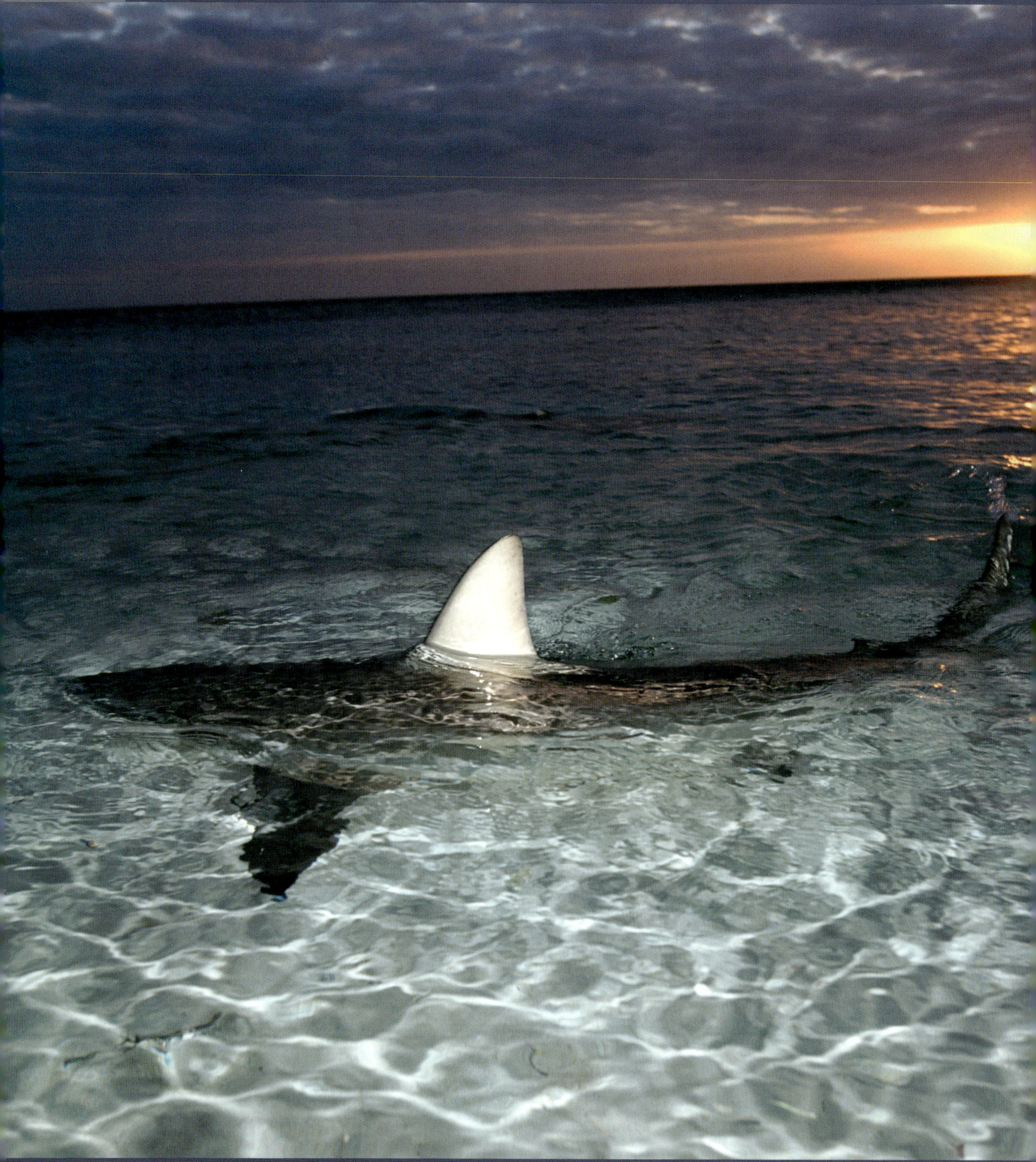

Many sharks like to hunt for food in shallow water

Sharks live in every ocean of the world. Most sharks live in warm water. But some sharks live in cold water. Many sharks live in **shallow** water near land. But some live in deep water in the middle of the ocean.

shallow not deep

Most sharks eat fish and squid. Some big sharks eat turtles, sea lions, and dolphins. A few kinds of sharks eat tiny, floating plants and animals.

Sharks like to find big groups of fish they can eat

13

14

Some mother sharks lay egg cases. Others give birth to live babies. Shark babies are called pups. Most mother sharks leave the pups after they are born. Sharks can live 20 to 30 years in the wild.

A shark's egg case can look a lot like a plant

Sharks have to keep swimming all the time. Otherwise they will sink. Some sharks swim very far. They can swim thousands of miles every year!

Sharks move all the time but usually swim slowly

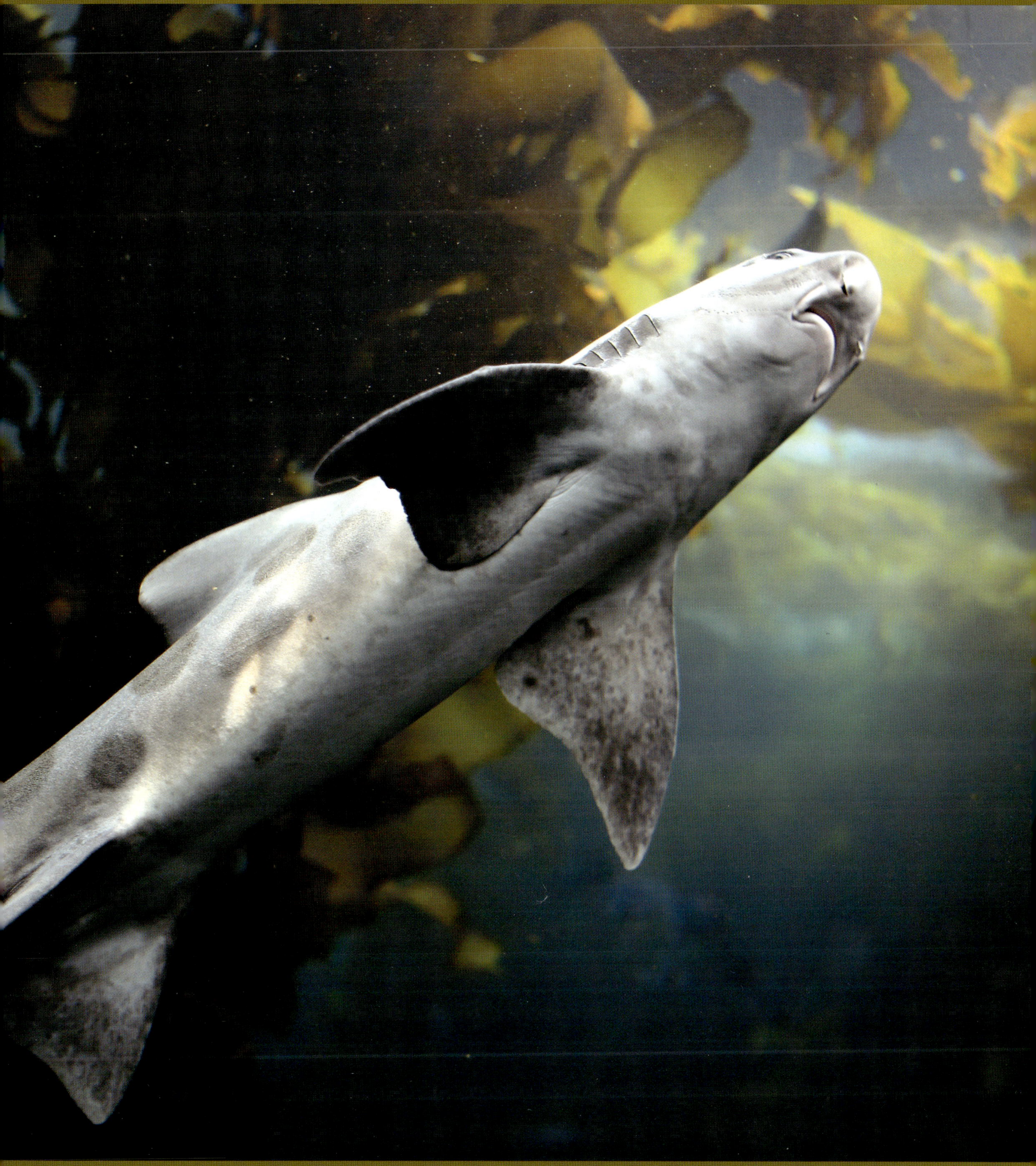

SHARKS

18

Sharks spend most of their time hunting for food. Some kinds of sharks hunt alone. Others hunt in groups called schools.

Hunting sharks are good at smelling blood in water

People can get close looks at sharks at aquariums

Many people are afraid of sharks. But most sharks will not hurt people. Most people will never see a shark in the ocean. But people can watch sharks at zoos and **aquariums** (*uh-KWARE-ee-ums*). It is exciting to see these strong fish swim through the water!

aquariums buildings where fish and other water animals are kept in big tanks

21

A Shark Story

Why do sharks have a bump on their head? People in a place called the Cook Islands used to tell a story about this. They said that one day, a shark let a girl named Ina ride on his back. The girl wanted to open a coconut. She cracked it on the shark's head. She hit him so hard that she made a bump on his head. The bump is called "Ina's bump"!

Read More

Lindeen, Carol. *Sharks*. Mankato, Minn.: Capstone Press, 2005.

Shea, Therese. *Sharks*. New York: PowerKids Press, 2007.

Web Sites

Enchanted Learning: Sharks
http://www.enchantedlearning.com/subjects/sharks/index.html
This site has lots of facts about sharks.

KidZone Sharks
http://www.kidzone.ws/sharks
This site has shark facts, activities, and pictures.

Index

aquariums 20
cartilage 7
egg cases 15
food 12, 19
gills 7
hunting 19
oceans 11, 20
pups 15
size 8
swimming 16
teeth 7
zoos 20